NIGHT TRAVELS

BY

CHRISTOPHER KUHL

Night Travels
Copyright: Christopher Kuhl
Published: August 2017
ISBN: 978-0-692-89488-0

Cover design by Self-Publishing Relief
This book was published with the assistance of Self-Publishing Relief, a division of Writer's Relief.

Some poems included in this volume first appeared in the following publications:
"Letting Go," *Schuylkill Valley Journal of the Arts*, 2013
"I Must Be Mad" and "Three Moments," *Glass: A Journal of Poetry*, 2013
"Nocturne," *Alabama Literary Review*, 2013
"Thoughts When I Was Younger" and "Writing Matters," *Red Ochre Press*, 2014
"Sera di Verano" and "The Tenth Year: Prayer," *Griffin*, 2014
"Body and Soul" and "Beginnings," *OVS Magazine*, 2014
"Morton Arboretum on a Saturday Afternoon," *Crack the Spine*, 2015
"Simple Poem," *OxMag*, 2015
"Trapped in the Wrong Skin," *Stickman Review*
"Passing Through," *Forge*, 2016
"Night Travels," *Burningword Literary Journal*, 2017
"Us. Them." *El Portal*, 2017

Published by Beaver Creek Press
© Christopher Kuhl, 2017

In The Beginning

In the beginning when God created the heavens and the earth, the earth
was a formless void and darkness covered the face of the deep; darkness
was all, everywhere. How did we know we weren't in a black hole, or in
a gap in the galaxies, the constellations

the stars we could not see because there was no light, and humans had
yet to be made, to see and love the stars? Darkness covered the face of
the earth, and humans, made of the dust of the earth, now worked in
the earth, presuming to make that light which God had yet to bring
forth, digging for coal, drilling for oil, extracting kerosene from wood and
shale—

searching for a meaningful life on the face of the earth. Beneath the
surface, fire churned, molten rock and fire burst through the earth's
crust as volcanoes, rushing down mountains all over the earth, running
the earth's rivers of blood, the sky ash-black and gritty, destroying what
God had made for humankind: was this the light? We lay prostrate,

while a wind from God swept over the face of the waters. This was the
darkness, the void, the Voice, begotten not made, and we, bones and
flesh, burnt and buried in the clay, could not open our eyes to see what
was no longer there.

For Monica

LOOKING OVER THE EDGE

You have to have
The power over lonesomeness
To live out here
In a plank house in hill country
In the middle of nowhere. No

Barn, no fence; a collapsing
Porch. Nothing but an old,
Rusted-out Dodge in the ditch,
Beneath a blood-dark, starless sky.

TABLE OF CONTENTS

POEM: ONE WORD A STORY MAKES

Decadent.

A quality of a person, style, act...

A dish of blueberries
With fresh cream and sugar.

Each word a story in itself
And in common with each other...

My blueberries. Your blueberries.

Each one of us a different life,
A different reader, always changing,

Relishing

A different universe...

NOCTURNE

(for Barbara Gavin in memory of Tom Gavin)

I heard the sea pounding
pounding the sea pounding on the rocks
dashing against them:
I heard it and my ears were filled with the pounding
and the rocks and the sea

and in the morning
I arose and went down to the sea's rough edge
and I touched that edge where the night had touched it
and I remembered the sea dashing
dashing against the rocks

MORTON ARBORETUM ON A SATURDAY AFTERNOON

Two women walk
A path together. They

        stop,

and ask me
to take their picture.

But then an old couple
steps up, closer

to them and does it.

        Really,

on this blue, shining day,
I would have been touched,

happy to help.

THREE MOMENTS

the darkest night
     then light
          the scent of lilacs

*

     Gettysburg winter
     the sky hangs with bitter stars
     a bloody drum pounds—

*

     two cats sleeping
          curled back to belly
              breathing together

THE PRESENT PAST

What is the world? Water,
Wind, dirt, fire. We look up
From Earth, sometimes with telescopes,
And see galaxies light-years away:

We're seeing their past,
What happened there
Millions of years ago: living,
Breathing history. And somewhere,

Millions of light-years from us,
Some poor SOB sees us as
We really aren't: history in
The present in the past-present,

Galactic fields of billions of
Stars. No one ever sees the future:
There is none, which we all know
Sometimes. We are locked in the present,

The only escape a jailbreak of
Memories. That is all we have;
Today's news is yesterday's present,
Light-years from where we will never be.

MELANCHOLIA

Between memory and dream
There is no here and now:

Just something said from time to time,
Melancholy as a hoot owl, places

Marked by the names of families
Whose histories I do not know.

                     The stones, the stones,

Even the stones have eyes, but I,
Merely the shadow of a man,

See nothing. I am blind:
I used to think I remembered

Everything, but now I know
I don't. I have no memories,

Just dreams masquerading
As realities I could not, cannot live,

                     But in which I once believed,

Sure as breathing. (Between memory
And dream, there is no here and now.)

BODY AND SOUL

A doe, alive with an unborn fawn,
Lies beside
The road, legs shattered.

The mother must learn,
With only this moment, to choose
To find the strength

To die, to let the fawn
Die, too. So must we all,
When the moment comes, choose

To embrace our mortality,
Shattered strength and all,
As well as the fawn, the dreams within.

FADING

What do old men dream about?
What are the dreams of old women?

The old men

Sit on the back steps,
A glass of whiskey on the step below,
In easy reach.

The old women

Sweat in the kitchen, frying up cornpone
And side meat for their quiet, lonely supper:
The kids are grown and gone their ways

And the old men and old women
Wish they had something to talk about.
But after all this time—

It's been nigh on sixty years—
Dreams have become just faded memories.

Yet still, at bedtime

The old men and the old women
Curve into each other. And maybe
That's the dream they've been living,
In lean times and fat.

Lord Almighty, God bless them all.

ARMISTICE DAY

(and your young men shall see visions,
and your old men shall dream dreams)

*

A million bodies
rotting in the mud, dead—

      wherever the corpse, there the vulture—

dead

bayonets, cannons, mortars,
machine guns, mustard gas:

      neither bones nor bodies will flourish in the grass:

there is no grass, no Ezekiel,
just miles of trenches, broken fields
knee-deep in shattered arms, legs, faces;
no tombstones, just the gray debris
of what was once human...

      Oh, tell me, where is the honor, the glory?

A generation lost, no longer
do we contemplate the mystery, the miracle of life;
rather, death consumes us all

(which has its own mysteries):

a world forever lost in the fields of moon,
fields of blood, and a blood moon hanging

JERUSALEM

What is a man to a tethered colt?
What is a colt to a dying man?

My brother, in the raw indecency
Of blood, ten million men walk in

Our bones. And yet we are too insignificant
To cast a shadow of our own.

But Christ

Crucified cast a deep shadow over
The whole world, a shadow, then light

Even the fiery pit could not and cannot equal.

My brother, you are tired.
Close your eyes, and see.

Night Travels

PSALM

My soul, the blood that ties me
To my place,

The blood that runs through the people
Of my town

Runs through me.

Praise His Holy Name,

Cry out with joy. As the deer longs
For water,

So longs my soul for You, O God,
So longs my soul.

Flesh, blood:

Go find yourself, lost boy, beyond the hills,
Toward home.

The path may be dark now,

The dark night terrifying, but know this:
Soon the light will come;

It will come forever. Praise His Holy Name.

MY WISH, MY LOVE

I want to play the cello. I dream
Of Yo-Yo Ma playing Schubert,
But I am too fat:

Unable to wedge the cello between
My knees, it would rest perilously,
Teetering on my ample belly.

                    I would be unable

To draw my bow fully across the strings,
Or reach the fingerboard's far end
Without suffocating.

If only I could play the cello
At sunset, bringing forth the music
Of the spheres,

I might fall in love
With a large, ruddy, redolent woman
To make love with as lyrical and mellow

As any music or instrument ever heard.

WRITING MATTERS

The problems of beginnings
and ends.

For that matter, middles
to hold one's attention

once you've hauled the reader in.
And then

the difficulty of finding
a fulfilling end.

Really,

beginnings, middles and ends
are all meat—although vegetables will do,
if you prefer—

something to chew on,
gristle, bone, and all.

SCATTERED STARS, NIGHT WATERS

I look at my hands:
They're my mother's, my grandmother's.
Surely, they can't be mine:
Ropy blue veins, shifting wrinkles,
Age spots.

A deep grief chokes me.

Now that they're gone,
Keeping me from saying the words
That would help, as I sit
In the dark, staring at the river,
The manic scattering of stars
Rising above the night waters.

We don't inherit from,

We become our elders, whom we cannot
Remember as ever young; no longer
Believing in our own immortality,
We rub our hands mindlessly over
And over, in the outer darkness,

Then place them quiet, still,
In our ancient laps.

A LAZY MAN'S POEM

What I saw:

A chilly, raw Wednesday,
An old man walking up the sidewalk,
Bent into the wind, eating
A vanilla ice-cream cone.

What I didn't see:

A chilly, raw Wednesday,
An old man walking up the sidewalk,
Bent into the wind, eating
A vanilla ice-cream cone.

What is real? What is a riddle?
What does anyone know?

RIDDLES

How many handfuls of dust must be gathered
Before there is one planet?

How many gasses must be ignited
Before there is one sun?

How many drops of rain must fall
Before there is a creek, a river, many rivers,

An ocean?

And how many kings must be elevated
Before there is one King, one Word?

How many people must wander in the desert,
Generation after hungry generation,

Before there is one people, one world,
Singing joyfully for their covenant,

Praying and worshipping the Name
Of the maker of that covenant?

And how many peoples, nations must be broken
Before the One returns?

There are many questions, many unknown answers
Flowing in the Universe. But when will they be answered?

What is big and red and eats rocks?

Really, we are mere children,
And the question is meaningless.

Night Travels

Physics Lesson

You think your hand
Is flat, slapped on the table,
But it isn't completely:

Electromagnetic force
Keeps your hand from going through,
For the table, like us,

Is mostly space.
Atoms themselves are mostly space,
Except for a dense center,

We throw a spear to kill,
And it continues to fly through space,
Achieving escape velocity;

Yet the man is dead,

Tethered by present gravity
In a universe of mostly space, darkness
And fallen light.

LIBIDO

I sit on my patio,
A cup of coffee in my hand.
In the parking lot

A robin stands,
Occasionally grooming himself,
While looking around.

At grass's edge,

A female emerges and hops
To him. They circle, each grooming
The other, until he comes

From behind and mounts her.
She raises her tail feathers,
They both flutter a bit,

Preen a little more

And then separate and wing away,
Out of sight. I ask myself,

Birds thrive under the rainbow;
Why then, oh why can't I?

Night Travels

ALAMO

We breathe together, clinging
To one last frontier.
Flags in the dust,

        We crouch behind a wall.

I know a little
Of what you are thinking: Davy Crockett,
Jim Bowie,

        The Alamo! What passions

Did history push aside
Until nothing was left but a few stones,
The remnants of a scuffle...

        What will happen to us? How long

Before we are reduced
To dates, statistics, theories? How will we remember
Anything, anything at all?

        (Perhaps there is a wisdom

In things; it is easier to remember love
As a tatter of cloth,
A yellow petal, a late-night sigh

        And death—

An overshoe,
A threadbare jacket,
Outriders from the western skies)

THE TENTH YEAR: PRAYER

Next month it will be ten
years. A poet once said grief
is precisely the weight

of a sleeping child, but
how would I know? I am
that grieving child. As I stand

in the cold, quiet graveyard,
wild birds skim the western sky,
the sun sets, the wind

rises. Even the stones rear up:

Oh, surely

souls live; they must,
surely they must. Mother,
hear me, help me breathe.

A SIMPLE POEM

My hair came out in tufts.
I looked like a beat-up old
Stuffed bear. I felt beat up.

But then

My brother stepped in:
He shaved my head clean,
Worked lotion into my scalp,

And I knew that he loved me.

NIGHT TRAVELS

Curving, climbing, descending
On steel tracks, the moon keeping pace
While in ten thousand little towns
The sleepers sleep in the earth.

        In ten thousand furious days,

Men, machines, explosives
Blast through the mountains,

Hard labor building highways: the age
Of the motorcar has come and must

Be accommodated. But there are
No real rules yet, and whether

In a plush Pullman smoking car, or a flivver
In a field, men will hop up, pulling

Long and deep from jugs of corn whiskey.
The ten thousand days diminish one

By one, and trains, men, swaying,
Drunk, join the sleepers of the little towns;

        Sleep, while mountains and fields

Shift and change from what they once
Knew them to be, and cannot, even now,

In their stertorous breathing, imagine

        The stranglehold to come.

A LEPER'S TALE

A cheap book:
Smeared

Ink, old pages that
Smell

Like fish, cheese, yeast—

An infection
Without the itch to read,

Know more, tell more or less,

Rather,

No matter how despicable the
Body, how vile the subject,

Everything
Still clots. My eyes, belly, limbs
Itch, smell like

Spoiled ricotta. Turn the page
If you desire;

Turn away from me if you must.
It's not my job to make you comfortable.

VISIONS

The whole town
Has been swallowed up
By a forest. The only clear spots

Are the old cemetery: my final
Resting place, but not yet:

Not yet—

>   (The trees have great respect for the dead,
>   even the dying on their long journey into a
>   future that does not/cannot/will not ever, in
>   any meaningful way, exist)

—And the parking lot at
St. Stephen's, although
Most people walk to Sunday Mass.

>   This is my town, the forest people

My people, my blood,
Now and forever.

THOUGHTS WHEN I WAS YOUNGER

1.

Teachers
lived at school. At night
they did long division,
conjugated verbs,
and then slept under their desks.

2.

Priests
wore black pajamas with Roman collars
to bed, and slept in cells
full of votive candles
from which they lit their cigarettes.

3.

My dad, a trucker,
drove back and forth across
the country, sniffed diesel,
drawled on the CB radio,
and drove a million miles a year.

4.

My siblings and I
were born by immaculate conception: my parents
whispered for hours behind closed doors,
and then my father emerged, beaming,
and my mother was fat.

MUSINGS: ANOTHER YEAR

It's real. We always knew
It was real, inevitable,
But we couldn't, wouldn't believe it,
Not us: we were young;
It didn't apply.

And then suddenly

We're sixty. Maybe
We have another ten,
Twenty,

Maybe even thirty years left.
Or maybe we won't get past sixty. And
If we do, what condition will we be in?

I was wondering aloud

About heaven and hell one day,
And a woman twenty, twenty-five years my senior
Told me to shut up:
It was coming soon enough.
We always knew, but now—

No, it's self-indulgent to live in fear.
It's coming, so go about your
Ordinary days. Live in peace.

A SHY POET

(In memory of L. Cohen)

He sang songs about grief,
Freedom, love, the lost:

He remembered those left
Amidst the garbage and the

Flowers, about Jesus as a sailor when
He walked upon the water. But

The poet has died, and we,
The ancient young, are crushed:

We sit shiva, praying his words,
Chanting his songs:

Hallelujah! Hallelujah!

DEATH OF A MAN

He is dying. One minute
He is fat, giving me wet willies,
And then, the next, his belly is gone.

He does not speak. He grins,
Teeth clamped in pain, the muscles
Along his jaw and neck strained,
The outlines of his skull surrounding
His dark, drooping, denying eyes:

He's dying in plain sight. I do not
Know him well, and what I see

Is the body's mockery of what it means
To return to our ancestors. Sometimes,
If you're lucky, you get a second chance. But here,

His skull and wasted frame give it away:
He is doing this dying only once,
And for keeps.

LENTEN JIHAD

Ring around the rosies,
Pockets full of posies—

The fading, slow melt
Of winter;
The chaos of the coming
Spring.

Ash Wednesday. The ongoing
Jihad, year after year struggling,
Drawing ever closer to our God—

            Ashes, ashes, we all

Fall down.

GOOD FRIDAY

Darkness is grief is darkness
Is love is mercy is love
Is blood is water is blood—

We breathe, struggling to exhale,
Swallowing to breathe,
But we forget how to swallow,

How to break the knots in
Our lungs: if we fail,
We die and the light dims

And is gone. Yit' gadal v'yit
Kadash sh'mei raba. Omaine

(May His Great Name grow exalted and sanctified. Amen)

Early Snow, Leaves

Two dried-up leaves, huddling
Edge to edge, body
To body, hanging on in the variable
Winds. Then a strong gust

Blows them apart, sends them
Skittering:

They're gone, leaving no mark
On the crusted snow,

No memory of their ever existing—

Lost, 1941

1.

crashing through the woods
dense as an internment camp

screaming

soul reduced to ashes—

brother,

bring me home

2.

the supermoon shines
rising in the eastern sky

smoke, grit:

a train rolls through

3.

a spark of fire quickening
threatening

in the night

in the night:

my heart contracts—

my feet crushing hollow bones

Night Travels

ANCIENT TIMES. MODERN TIMES. WINTERTIME.

Spiky bird tracks in the snow,
Like cuneiform tablets, wedges
Recording business, laws, literature
Of the ancient Sumerians.

We, too, have our own cuneiform:
The spiky music of Stravinsky, Prokofiev, Bartók:
Sharp colors, angular rhythms
Yet lyrical, too, lovely as a heartbeat relaxing.

               The weather here

Has been in the deep freeze,
Two feet on the ground:
Not lyrical at all; rather, dissonant
As we freeze in our wedged tracks.

               Then suddenly,

We're in the upper thirties.
The snow begins to melt, steaming away
Any mark of our presence. I wish I could read
Cuneiform. I wish a bit of it

In my coat pocket, a bit of clay
That I could scratch back, wishing them well,
And sharing our spiky times:
The Firebird, Lt. Kijé;

And most of all, world to world,
Ancient to new, the *Mikrokosmos,*
Musical cuneiform steaming.

NORTH COUNTRY HARVEST

Mid-September. The farmer
Back of us is running his combine
And trucks through the fields,
Chopping corn, getting it ready
For Farney and Steiner's feed mill.
It's been a hot, dry summer, and
The combine and field trucks raise up
A hell of a lot of dust.

A hell of a lot of dust.
We've been sitting out back,
Talking and drinking coffee,
And we're a little dusty ourselves.

In fact, my paper is a little dusty
And my pen scratches as I write this.

BURN DOWN THE MOUNTAIN

The wildfire burns off
      All the trees, brush;
Burns the mountain down.

Is it the world's end?
      The waterlogged earth
Runs off, triggering mudslides.

Bodies are suddenly, helplessly
      Twisted, bent, entombed
For eternity as we know it.

A white wooden cross
      Stands planted at the base,
A prayer for the unknown lost.

HUNGER

When I was young, at family gatherings
I was afraid. I didn't recognize these people,
With their ancient accents and woolens
Musty even in summer, their old and
Rheumy eyes grabbing at me. But

I didn't take refuge in my mother's
Skirts, or run shouting and screaming
With the other children. I was told
They were my cousins, but I did not feel
A connection; I did not feel safe.

So I sought out my father,
Standing behind and gripping his
Long, straight legs, peering out once in a while,
Secure with his hand on my head or shoulder.

I was my father's cub, not, like my sister,
His princess; nor would I grow up to be king:
That was my brother's future. Rather,
I would be a bear like my father, watching
The plates of food being passed, hungry,

But too afraid to eat in this foreign nest
Of women, children, and old men chewing cigars.

FATHERS AND SONS

The young boy listens
To his father's words;
His father does not know

How hard the boy listens.

But the boy wants to be
A man like his father
When he grows up, and so

He hangs on every word,
Sentence, every paragraph,
Every story. Much

Of it he will hear again

And again from grandfathers, uncles,
Cousins, and other family

He does not know.

But the truth of it all
Lies in the timbre and
Cadence of his father

Speaking, teaching him
Without knowing how profoundly,
Right through their entangled lives,

The truth that lies
In the deep night's light of a
Shivering moon,

The deep truths shared by father and son.

MIXED QUARTET

1.

What is this place, and why am I here? My ancestors do not lie in graves in the small town's small church cemetery. I was not born here; I hope I do not die here, although as exhausted and three-quarters starved as I am, I just might. And who will bury me? Who will come looking for me? Who will recite a hymn for me, or sing a lonesome song for me? I have no money and only the tattered clothes I wear. They will bury me in an unmarked pauper's grave. I will die, and in death I will have no name.

2.

It seems a hard way to end. Years of children and houses and gardens and bills to pay and days so busy it seemed that we would finally wear out; all our frictions, our tensions would erase us; we would simply disappear into an exhausted nothingness—

A hole in the earth's atmosphere, a spot of negative energy.

Instead, here we are—

Living out days we dreamed about, a nightmare we never saw coming.

The things we want to end never do, and the things we want to last forever have a way of fading even before we get there. And we? We just go on, living out our days, an average of all motion, a summary of changes.

We stay in one place,

Turning as the earth turns and all that changes passes around us, lost in the light-years, millions of them, to a vanishing point in the universe.

3.

Contamination. Contagion. Small tragedies that combine to the biggest and wipe out a town from diphtheria. Children first in the mass grave, covered with blankets and shovels of dirt. Then adults, digging and sickening, and falling in and covered like the children. There is no weeping, no wailing: everyone is too sick, weakened, dying; the only sound is the shovels scraping.

Until finally all, except for one man,

Are dead. He finishes filling the grave, crosses himself, and leaving no marker, walks away, until suddenly he falls dead by an old pine. A man with no name—they're all lost, nameless— blackened houses, burnt, the town gone, leaving behind the odors of smoke, dirt, decay, and dead leaves. Putrefaction. Even the light is fading: no moon tonight and rumors in other towns of the devil here, a massive sin, impervious to exorcism, healing.

4.

This is a part of the country that has no speed limits. He'd seen 50, 60 mph, but no limit? Never. And yet he found it both wonderful and terrible, scary: why crawl at 60 mph and take six hours to get to where he really wanted to be, than to run at 100, 110 mph, and get there in three? And who has the experience, the hands, the rage to control the car at the pinnacle of its power? Seventy, eighty are dangerous even now, wrangling around the occasional vehicles on the almost empty road. But then to die alone in a limitless run to nowhere, a speed where even the smallest tic of steering or lapse of attention cries out savage and cruel, and every bone in his body is broken, and blood pours out of his ears and nose, eyes and throat,

All alone in the middle of nowhere.

Nobody will notice him until an hour, two hours, when a pickup comes and finds him, and he's dying and they know it, but there's nothing anybody can do but stare as he looks up, his gray eyes glazed with red, and then he dies, is dead, and the men lift him into the back of the truck, and hopeless, take this boy first to a local doctor, really a horse doctor is all they have, and then silently take the body, the young man's dead body, to the gravedigger's, and then they walk away and do what the young man can do no longer:

Breathe, breathe, in and out,

Steady as he goes.

GOATS

Kids are small people.
Goats are big kids

Men with long mustaches
And chin hair have goatees.

Mothers on farms love
And bottle-feed their littlest goaties.

Kids love to scramble in
The dirt with their goaties,

I have the beginnings

Of a wispy goatee. My father's
Is a full, dark goatee.

I never grew up; instead
I look like a big goat,

But inside I am a little kid,
Face smeared with dirt

So for a few minutes
I can have a goatee,

Kid that I am.

MEMORIES

1.

Mine are not yours,
Though we grew up in the
Same house, siblings with the
Same fighting—always fighting—
Parents, taking turns assaulting us
Until we all were exhausted, reduced
To silence. The fighting parents
Drifted up to their bedroom, slammed
The door, and suddenly,

All would be quiet.

2.

As children, we did not talk
To each other; we knew we were all
Under some force, some fate,
But it wasn't the same for each of us.

3.

When we were adults, we did not
Talk; rather, we drifted silently
Away from each other, from what,
Even though having been confined,
Incarcerated in the same space, was
Never a family. Military grunt work
Was a relief; too much booze, DUIs
And jail were a relief; flipping burgers
Was a relief; death was a relief—anything
So as not to have to talk to one another—

Night Travels

Was a relief. Anything. My memories
Were not yours:
You would never understand—

4.

And now, all but one of us
Are in our fifties and sixties,
All of us but the last child, born
To be a peace offering after
We all left. What does he
Understand? I am the eldest,
He seventeen years younger, and
I am ashamed:

I do not understand him;
Everything I say to him is wrong,
Although I try now to be a
Big brother. He's having none
Of it: he bears my father's name,
Yet never knew him. How could he
Understand what came before?

5.

We organize our memories,
Make new stories: there is no
DNA match; rather, only remnants
Of skin and bones, sinews, sucked
Into a black hole, the total annihilation
And silencing of light,

The silencing of what never was or will be

BEFORE I WAS BORN (BUT CANNOT FORGET)

Mass graves in the forest. Those
Who can still stand wield a shovel,
Pushing the bodies into bloody,
Muddy, suppurating, helter-skelter
Piles. The dead, their souls

Torn from their bodies, never to return,
Live in the shadows of another world,
A black hole, starving for the light.

All the world is at war,
Yet not everybody realizes the
Atrocities going on from Germany to Poland,
China to Russia, to the Ukraine and Japan.
Not just Jews and troops and POWs,
But others, their plain lives snatched
Away, sixty to eighty million
Dead.

Dead. Still, when I visit Yad Vashem
And see the thousands of artifacts,
And the dome covered with pictures
Of the murdered Jews, something inside me
Breaks: How can I say these words?

Glorified and sanctified be God's great name
Throughout the world which He has created
*According to His will...*yada yada yada...
How can I believe?

I stand in the center and scream,
And hear the cattle cars creaking again,
Laden with those already lost, too numb
To cry, to pray.

LETTING GO

1.
Verdict

You have hurt me,
bled me, taken my voice,
broken my heart. I have
suffocated, but no more:

I will take back

my voice, my power;
you are ashes: I will stake
a bloody, torn, thorn-encrusted rose

on your grave: my foe,
you are dead to me forever.

2.
Message

A wise and holy woman
said to me, listen for peace
after anger: God's will,
not yours. Anger—

3.
The Last Word

—will eat you alive. Know
she has joined the ashes of the
Holocaust. It's over:

You are living, breathing.
A blessing upon you:
Shalom.

QUESTIONS

Now I take the long journey,
Ospreys signaling imminent danger:

Pelican Mother, Pelican Father, let us die,
Then dig your beak into your feathered breast,
Spill the blood into our mouths

And bring us back to life.

                    Bring us back to life. As the words flow,

I am unable to focus on the Gospel,
The homily; somehow
They are a foreign language and I

                    Am in a strange land, caught

Between earth and sky. Why do I write?

I write because I'm angry, so angry I can't pray; because my
people have left me, far away, because I have nowhere to go. I
write because the pen is sharper than the knife, ink flowing like
blood, prints smearing, smearing with each heartbeat. How can
you leave? I write because I cannot go where you go, because
"until a man is nothing, God can make nothing of him."* The
pelican hovers; I weep.

*Martin Luther

POETRY: FROM CREATION TO REVELATION

The Garden. Did she talk
To the deer there? After all,
What did she have to say
To Adam? He was busy
With the Creation's inventory,
And his words were just nouns,
No verbs, conjunctions, moods,
No adverbs, adjectives, interrogatives
To glorify and understand this amazing
Place and carry on a dinner conversation.
So they chewed steadily, silently—
Nothing at all.

Eve was lonely. She took
Adam's nouns and tried to make
A language: sentences, questions,
Paragraphs. She talked to the
Earth and plants and shady
Trees and the River. And then
Someone said, "Talk to me, Eve,
And I will tell you things
Beyond Adam's ken." That someone
Was the Serpent, and he wove
A lovely, lacey web of conversation. Eve
Was enthralled: this beat Adam's words
Any day. So how could she resist
When he spoke a poem—the first poem
In history—to her about the fruit of
The Forbidden Tree in the center of the Garden?

After all,

She would like to be like God, with
Endless hours of conversation! But instead,
She realized she and Adam were naked,

Night Travels

Were not God. And she realized, for the first time
That words could be deceiving, especially
Poems. O God, God, God!
What was wrong after all with silence,
Broken only by a man with nothing but nouns,
No more to say, and obliviously, happily naked?

RUNWAY

Maple. Silver birch. Sycamore.
Ash. Aspen. Oak.

All deciduous,

They lose their leaves, shivering
In the autumnal equinox

And air.

But the mighty oak
Is last, layering its leaves,

Splendid,

On the fallen leaves of the other trees,
Slicking the paths, the roads,

A slippery surprise
To a pickup gunning its engine;

To a deer trying to run without falling,
Fleeing dogs

And armed, neon-vested men.

Somewhere nearby,
Squirrels leap effortlessly branch

To branch; crows
Argue, stone-hearted, oblivious
To the nude trees, fashionista models in the deep forest.

On The Edge

A tree's filigreed branches
Etch the dark sky, roseate
Against the streetlights.

It's quiet, the normally active street
Silent except for the occasional car
Hissing along the wet pavement.

This is the end

Of autumn, the beginning of winter:
Snow threatens.

BEGINNINGS

A boy and a girl,
Twelve, maybe thirteen,
Walking slowly, engaged
In conversation,

But not touching,
Although I can see
In their tentative bodies
That they want to. This

Is the scary, yet sweet
Beginning of a journey
To what the future might be,
Although maybe not with

This particular boy
And this particular girl.

TRAPPED IN THE WRONG SKIN

Barbie for a girl
Who is really a boy, who
Dismembers it,

And smashes it

With a rock,
Burying the pieces in scattered stones,
Sticks and leaves.

The parents

Panic. The grandmother says
The girl-boy
Is possessed by a demon.

The whole family

Panics. But in an old *Reader's Digest*
The girl-boy finds
An article on "transsexuals"

And is relieved

Not to be alone, to have a name; yet scared:
How will the girl-boy
Make the change?

S/he bites

Her arm hard, and
Boy's blood springs up shining, bright.
But the girl is eight,

And doesn't know

Night Travels

About the blood coming in a few years
(Although s/he's heard voices):

It will shatter

The girl-boy: thick, pulpy, ropy
No longer sweet, bright, free-flowing
Boy blood.

S/he howls

And picks up a razor blade.
Only the girl-boy can save himself,
Only the boy,

Someday, hopefully

A man

NOBODY KNOW WHY

"Seems like we're just set down here, and don't nobody know why."

—a woman to Annie Dillard

This is what life is:

First you struggle up from your tangled sleep;
Then a shower,
Jeans and a t-shirt,
Coffee,

And you begin walking

Down through the park, a hill, a vacant lot—
And then past houses,
Radios murmuring *sotto voce* from open windows,
Music,

And your legs are strong

And you're striding,
The streets glimmering from the heat already.
Sweat seeps between your shoulder blades
In this city of sleepers,

And you think "I am walking and breathing, and that is called living,

But I do not know why I am."

THREE PRAYERS

1.

Walking a still path, I come upon
Blood, feathers, bone

Everywhere: nature's violence.
Pray for the soul ascending.

2.

The river of God
Is full of water. Drink deeply:

There are no wells.
Cup your hands and pray for the thirsty.

3.

Autumn winds.
Leaves scrabble along the sidewalk

Like crabs at the beach.
Pray for the seasons, for life after death.

ONE SENTENCE

The clean green scent of grass
Coarse grass telling us with its clean
Green scent that winter is behind
Us, spring ready to pounce, the rain
Falling, the grass thickening, needing
Mowing, the new shoots filling in
Patches, the suicidal thoughts of winter
Gone,

The spring bounding, moving inexorably
After a few temperate nights into
The summer heat and muggy air
Tearing us between the flaming sun
Ready to explode and seeking refuge
In the comforts of air-conditioning,

But then the heat starts to falter—
Still plenty of ninety-degree days—
And the fields are gathered in, stored,
Eighty-degree days more frequent
Until the air starts to crisp,
The leaves turn, the nights breathe frost,
Autumn

With a full moon and changes of
Time, darkness coming early with
Skies of iron and pounding sleet
As the roads slick and winter comes,
Mountains of snow and ice, trapped,
Freezing in this longest season and
The wind's sharp tooth, bloodless
Balancing precariously in the endless
Dark, a sentence without end

RAIN

drizzle kids circling shrieking
downpours adults running newspapers
over their heads rain shooting
sideways like bullets blood against your
face hurricane-strength wind thunder
rain turning umbrellas inside out ribs
threatening to slash tearing the fabric
rain falling soaking the unprotected
rain spits off and on lightning
strikes threatening bare feet in a
muddy pool of rainwater dying down
dying down slowing to just a steady downpour
the sky turning black to gray
and then it stops and then there's the sun
and the clouds break the rain disappears
a soaker the air cooled but humid

sticky sticky sticky

SNAKE DREAM

In a muddy field

a grass snake lies
in the late sun and imagines himself
to be a great python:

he slithers quietly

up to, and then, mouth
wide open, seizes an unsuspecting cow,
and squeezing, relaxing, squeezing,

draws the cow
into his body, pressure and enzymes
pulverizing

bone, meat, sinew and tattered hide
into a soupy, bloody mess, until
he is sated—

Suddenly, he wakes

and sees the muddy cow standing,
and he knows that really he's doomed
to be no more than a grass snake

in a blackened, boggy field.

EARTH SCRIPTURES

earth

a leaf faded

the weight of shadow

perpetrator victim witness

earth alive as breathing bones

breathing bones white ash

splinters the laughter of the damned

laughter's waves reproaching the shore

the trinity land sea sky

earth's breathless winds

the burden of being

gravity tugging at the rock-bound earth

the living earth

Us. Them.

The word, the stone, the leaf.

Witch hazel.

The everlasting beat of time passing.

The smell of dry grass, leather.

Tobacco.

The fierce pleasures of whiskey.

War looms.

       War will always loom. And break out.

       In prehistoric times, small clans wandered.

       You were The People; the others were not.

       You killed them and you ate them.

Violence still rules.

Violence roams a world where no one is welcome.

We all are The People.

We all are the Other.

We do not eat each other anymore.

Buddhists, Jews, Christians, Muslims,

Night Travels

Latinos, Native Americans, Asians, Eastern Europeans

We shoot, we bomb, we burn.

We collect heads and put them on display.

I smother with rage and sorrow.

Maybe I will do what my brothers did before me.

Leave the world.

Go home to my people in the heart of the Adirondacks.

A SON'S INHERITANCE

A son inherits his father's voice
And pulls the sword out of the stone:

His is the force to be reckoned with now;
He has taken his share of reckonings, beatings,

Ordeals: everything to prove he is now
A man.

I have not inherited my father's voice,
But I have endured and learned his

Language, his story; I wear an old suit
Of his,

And now I am a man, seeing a new world
Through eyes his color, but a generation

Younger. The earth is no longer flat,
The oceans and sky are approachable.

We have walked upon the moon, landed
A rover on Mars;

Our fathers' sons, we have our own stories
And visions:

I live behind the mountains;
My father's blood sings loud in my ears.

ALL MIMSY WERE THE BOROGOVES

For a moment
        I had disappeared.
The world still steady,

I was invisible.

        The forest was dark
Where once it had been light;

The sky blackened,
        Rain fell, mean and surly,
But I stayed dry,

Dashing between the drops:
        No spear for me
To grip as the wind

Turned me inside out.
        Wind, rain, dark, light:
The world continued

To rotate, orbit,
        Swing on the galaxy's tail
And I? I was flipped

Invisible once again
        And sentenced in my dim,
Dark room—

(Beware the Jabberwock, my son)—

To what?

A WORLD IN PIECES

Razor-wire fences.

Borders closed, detention centers
Packed, loaves thrown in

Once daily, catch
As catch can: no miracles here.

We think, at least we are
Across the sea, far away. But

We have our own civil unrest:
Chicago, Baltimore, Ferguson, Miami, LA, on and on...

Where can we go?

O Wanderer, say a prayer for us,

All of us both perpetrators and victims
Lost in a world we hold at arm's length;

Say a prayer for the soul of a child
Dismembered, nameless, unloved, incomplete;

Yes, my baby, your baby, ours,
Lost in an urban lagoon.

TIME PASSING

Lately, as I go from family
House to family house, everything—
Rooms, yards, porches—

Seems smaller than I
Remembered. I grieve—
For what? Some sort of

Stable history, identity:
They have been taken from me.
The stories of my family

Have become myths,
Myths that tiptoe toward
A dark, watery light, our steps

Echoing in these houses built
By my forebears, until someday
The generations will die out,

The houses will hold strangers,
And there will be no one left
To tell our stories, nothing here

That defines me. I will have
To wait: I, too, will become a
Piece of history, my identity

Reestablished in the graveyard
On the hill looking over the river,
One once again with my tribe,

My tribe asleep as the river

Night Travels

Flows ancient and quiet,
Older even than this hill

That bears our silenced bones.

I Must Be Mad

I sit, I touch
No one.
I build little piles
Of stones around me,
Little piles
Of sticks and mud
And bits of bone. I make
A little hut. I shriek
Like Baba Yaga.

I must be mad.
If I had
A little white suit
I would bob up and down,
Tap my toes. I would
Put my fingers
In my mouth and smile
Like an idiot.
I would dance, legs akimbo,
Across your table. If you
Fluttered
Your hands like a moth
I might go into the garden
And find one
Beneath the lamp. Maybe
I would swallow it,

Or maybe I would pluck
Its wings, I must
Be crazy
To love you; there are
Certain things to
Consider: an egg

Night Travels

Broken in the carton, a shoe
Tossed by the side
Of the road. Wildflowers
For your mother. I kissed you

On the hill
When the milkweed was ripe
And your hair like straw.

Our lips
Stuck. Our lips stuck.

I must be mad. I prance
Around
My little hut, singing
Witchy songs. I feel
Like a toad. Right now
If I smashed
Into a wall at the speed
Of light
This would be just so much
Ink and paper. Just a spot
In the road,
A piece of slime. I must be
Crazy
To love you.

Death. Silence.

A last breath and gone,
Lost to the grave. The spirit leaves,
Willingly? Unwillingly? There is
Only the unknown, only future generations
Keeping the covenant made with God
Millennia ago, praise His Name.

Then there are prayers, blessings,
And then the handfuls of dirt,
Including a fistful from Israel.
Afterward, the mourners drift about
The cemetery, remembering those who
Went before. Soon the family will go
To sit shiva, and all will depart
The holy ground.

While the workers hoist their
Shovels and fill in the grave,
Quietly breathing prayers, blessings
Not just for this soul, but for all the dead,
Lost in a silence greater than themselves,
Which they have never heard,
Now, before, after.

A MOMENT IN TIME

Hannah, Jim and I
Are sitting in the living room,
Listening to Prokofiev. Conversation

Is slow and quiet;
The cats are settling in, and
The fire throws dim shadows

Around us. Things are comfortable,
Orderly. I know these people well
And love them, this house,

This part of the world. I am
a cat, content, fulfilled.

PASSING THROUGH

Hannah moves

At her own pace

In her house
With three cats
On Hunter Lane. A wasp

Crawls on an inside window;
She captures it with a can and a lid
And releases it out the front door,

As though bidding farewell
To an honored guest.

The air cools.

Hannah gets a glass of wine;
Clouds amass, gray,
Steady. She hears

Her neighbor outside
On the gravel road, skidding
Into his driveway.

The wind rises,

And it starts to rain.

NIGHT HUNT

Evening descends on the
Sun's tail, darkness and light
Competing, struggling. The man

Of the house dozes amidst the smoke
And crackling of the fire pit, a drink
By his hand, while the women talk quietly
About this and that—

                    Until suddenly

Gus the cat runs up,
A bunny in his jaws, and

We all scramble, spilling our drinks,
To catch him. He runs,
Dropping the kit, surprised
At our reaction,

The kit too small,
Too dead to be surprised,
As evening clamps down, clattering
Into place.

SHIFTING GEARS

                                        I move at Chicago speed

In Tennessee,
But I'm adjusting. The sun
Burns, hammers,

So I sit on the screened porch,
Cogitating...

                                        No point rushing

Into things.

Night Travels

FOR FRANK

The winter solstice. We are
Lost in the single digits projected
By the TV weatherman.
And these are the darkest nights

Of the year, the winds whipping,
The cold invading and bending
Our bones, pulling our shoulders in,
Our back hunched as if
To protect our souls.

Oh, but for a little warmth,
Light; a single flame growing
Night by night, until the menorah,
Fully ablaze, drives off the dark,
But still casts long shadows;

The Advent wreath, fully lit,
Drives off the dark, candles
Without shadows, lit
For a different purpose, a mystery
We try to understand, but can't.

Oh, send me back where I can
Smell the pine woods of home,
Blind in the depths of winter,
But home again, home

Finally.

AIKEN COUNTY

Late at night I lay
In bed, awake, half listening
To trains plowing slowly

On tracks near the river,
Cars clattering, shifting on the rails,
Almost silent, I'd gotten so used

To them. Night after night,
I never really heard anything

Until one January night,
A sudden flash of light, shattering, screaming

And then, heavier than air,
Chlorine gas sank into the valley
Where the people slept dark in the

Dark night, not knowing what was
Happening. Some never woke up.

Slowly, wordlessly, river and earth
Turned upside down, inside out. Someone
Up the line forgot to throw the switch

And two trains collided in a metallic embrace
Rendering forever unlivable a tiny hamlet
In South Carolina, 2005.

In Which I Go For A Walk

A brisk morning
In eastern Tennessee,
I dress, drink a couple cups
Of coffee, eat some yogurt,
Listen to "The Writer's Almanac"
On NPR, put on a sweater,
And go for a walk. Two cats
Trail behind me, and then
Veer off. Trees and plants
Are starting to blossom,
And my allergies kick in.

Still, the walk is not
Unpleasant. I walk to the end
Of Hunter Lane, turn left on
Indiana Avenue, struggling to
Reach the fire hydrant. Once
There, I turn, retracing my steps
Past the lane and go up to the
Intersection of Indiana and Court,
Where I rest briefly on
A low brick wall in the sun. Then I return

To the house. For these few moments,
I have walked around the surface
Of the earth, and am wheezing,
Thirsty. I hang up my sweater,

And let an unimpressed cat
Out the door.

IN PERPETUITY

I passed an old cemetery as I rode into town today. There was a big, new sign: "New Plots Now Available." And I wondered how that was possible.

Some of the tombstones' markings were long faded, no longer legible: even blind fingers were unable to trace out something, anything. Some stones had cracked and fallen over, never to be righted again.

Did nearly two centuries, with family members long gone, buried elsewhere, lead the cemetery's caretakers to exhumations here, removing boxes of nothing more than dust, thus making way for new business? Or are graves available in the same plot, one body on top of another, mostly bone?

It's hard to think about. Even the church, long abandoned, is for sale. Lives long left, forgotten, cemeteries and churches are surrounded by the noise of commercial developments, traffic. The noise is deafening, meaningless.

(I heard that King Richard III was found buried underneath layers of land, fields, parking lots, somewhere in weather-beaten England. Really, there is no *in perpetuity* here for anyone.

Ever.)

LORD WILLING &

A creek

      water rushing over

            tightlyspacedrocks

::

        surrounded on the banks

:by ferns   :stunted trees

     It almost looks like—

no, not quite—

     more like—

        no, not that, either.

It's October, too cold
to wade,

        but I know

what it's like & what it isn't

:Double Eddy   :Double Eddy

with its

     slabsofgranitegreatslabs   shadowed

   where

Night Travels

the crick

don't

rise—

And On The Sixth Day

God made Sevierville. He
Filled it with beat-up roads
And potholes, told the angels
Not to worry about the infrastructure—

Fashioned endless open shopping malls
And objectified Indians and massive
Traffic jams, and when it was done,
The LORD said, "Yea, verily, it is good."

Then he said, "I think I'll rest,
Have a brewsky, and tomorrow, on the
Seventh day, I will rejoice in the fruit
Of my labors,

And go shopping."
And God was well pleased.

(A TRUE STORY)

Coming up the driveway
I see a wild turkey in full
Display at the front door.

It doesn't acknowledge
The car's wheels crunching on gravel,
So I ask it, in my most

Dulcet tones, "Hey, boy, hey, buddy, buddy,
Would you like to join us for dinner tonight?"

THE END OF THE STORY

Autumnal rains fall,
Rain even the oldest women,
With their prodigious memories,
Have never seen.

The rains become rivers,

Running down to the sea.
This winter, the rivers
And seas will freeze,
Blackening the world,

The darkness of a moonless, eternal night.

Quietly,

I will let the leaves
Fall and cover me, saturate
My bones until, in this
Rugged backcountry

I will have turned to stone,
A pile of granite lapped
At water's edge, eroded by the rushing river.

So I whisper silently,

There is a story here,
But it is no longer mine to tell,
Nor yours to hear.

SERA DI VERANO

In the waning light of a summer evening, the extended family gathers. The youngest chase fireflies with jam jars; the adults play bocce, clicking in the dark. Siblings and cousins argue over the identity of rising constellations, while the elders murmur quietly in Italian, sipping amaretto.

We are no more,

this village, than a wide spot in the road. Headlights approach, reflect in the windows, and then are gone, red taillights shimmering in the dark, hot breeze.

ACKNOWLEDGMENTS

I would like to thank all my readers and audiences for their support of my work over the years. They have given me encouragement, affirmation, and helped me keep going even when I thought I couldn't write another line.

I would like especially to thank Frank Rutledge; Bev Sperry; Fr. Michael D. Rasicci; Maud Hannah Volk; John Blanpied; Paul Kuhl; Shobha Sinha; Monica Sisco; Susan Waller;the Open Sky Poets, led by magnificent poet Lynne Handy; Anne Veague and Kevin Moriarity at Waterline Writers Studio; and the gang at Limestone Tea and Coffee House, who provide a great working ambience complete with savory scones, and tons of good coffee.

A special thanks and love is due to poet Sharon Doubiago for "discovering" me, and serving as a gentle, kind, and effective mentor.

I also would like to thank the staff at Writer's Relief for helping me get my work out there; thanks to their efforts, I publish regularly in journals all across the country, and occasionally in Canada. You work magic!

Finally, I would like to remember the late Kay Kasberger, who first recognized who and what I was years ago (I hate to say how many), and started me down the path I have been traveling in various ways ever since. God bless her.

I'm sure I've forgotten someone, but if so, it was unintentional. To all, all of you I send my heartfelt thanks. Without you, this book would never have come to fruition. And that includes all the many poets I've read in books and journals. You all have, and continue to teach me so much.

Shalom.

9 780692 894880